Mind Over Madness

Strategies for Thriving Amidst Chaos

Dan Desmarques

22 Lions

Mind Over Madness: Strategies for Thriving Amidst Chaos

Written by Dan Desmarques

Copyright © 2024 by Dan Desmarques. All Rights Reserved.

No part of this publication may be reproduced or transmitted in any form or by any means, electronic or mechanical, including photocopy, recording, or any information storage and retrieval system now known or to be invented, without permission in writing from the publisher, except by a reviewer who wishes to quote brief passages in connection with a review written for inclusion in a magazine, newspaper, or broadcast.

Contents

Introduction   VII

1. Chapter 1: Workplace Rivalry   1
2. Chapter 2: Living the Dream Life   5
3. Chapter 3: The Limits of Knowledge   9
4. Chapter 4: The Dangers of Ignorance   13
5. Chapter 5: The Price of Excellence   17
6. Chapter 6: Bullying as a Symptom of Fear   21
7. Chapter 7: Rising Above Fear   25
8. Chapter 8: The Cost of Ignorance in Health Care   29
9. Chapter 9: The Silent Threat to Cognitive Health   33
10. Chapter 10: The Neurotoxic Effects of Fluoride   37
11. Chapter 11: Exposing the Fraud in Education   41
12. Chapter 12: Dealing with Provocation   45
13. Chapter 13: Childish Games of Stupidity   49
14. Chapter 14: The Puppeteers of Ignorance   53
15. Chapter 15: Dealing with Narcissists   57

16.	Chapter 16: Confronting the Darkness in Society	61
17.	Chapter 17: Breaking the Chains of Learned Helplessness	65
18.	Chapter 18: Why Creativity and Intelligence Go Unnoticed	69
19.	Chapter 19: The Fleeting Motives of the Unwise	73
20.	Chapter 20: Discovering Hidden Strengths	77
21.	Chapter 21: Wisdom in Chaos	81
22.	Glossary	85
23.	Bibliography	99
24.	Book Review Request	101
25.	About the Author	103
26.	Also Written by the Author	105
27.	About the Publisher	113

Introduction

In a world where intelligence is overshadowed by ignorance, where success is met with envy and hatred, and where the pursuit of knowledge is often misunderstood, one individual navigates the complexities of life with resilience and determination. "Mind Over Madness: Strategies for Thriving Amidst Chaos" delves into the personal journey of an author who faces the challenges of living a life that many secretly desire but few truly understand. Through encounters with haters, manipulative personalities, and the limitations of the average mind, the protagonist discovers the true value of intellect, perseverance, and self-esteem.

As the story unfolds, readers are invited to explore themes of resilience, self-discovery, and the pursuit of truth in a world filled with illusions and misconceptions. From confronting betrayal and psychological abuse to finding solace in solitude and contemplation, the protagonist's experiences offer profound insights into the complexity of human nature and the power of individual growth.

"Mind Over Madness: Strategies for Thriving Amidst Chaos" is a compelling exploration of the human experience that challenges perceptions and invites readers to reflect on the dynamics of success, intelligence, and personal fulfillment.

Chapter 1: Workplace Rivalry

"Are you competing with Marcelo?" asked the dean of one of the universities where I worked.

"Why should I compete with Marcelo when Marcelo has no teaching experience and I can get a job at any university I want because of my background?" I replied.

She looked at me with a stupid face because she couldn't understand the lack of logic in her own brain or that Marcelo was smearing my reputation with lies to get me fired.

Fortunately for Marcelo, most people are mentally retarded, so he succeeded in getting me fired. But I also got a much better job afterwards, as I knew I would.

This makes me wonder if it's worth getting mad at stupid people because they can't win. It is as if they make my life better by trying to make it worse. Without them, I would probably get lazy and not change jobs or write as many books as I have or have as many wonderful experiences in life.

On the other hand, karma does catch up with people, because another person smeared that dean's reputation and months later she disappeared. Probably the bitch who took her place got rid of the dean with the help of the communist government because she spoke out against the political party.

Meanwhile, every single university I worked at was better than the one before, offering me a higher salary, a better reputation, and many more opportunities to meet interesting people and write better books. There are a lot of great things in my life that wouldn't happen without bad people.

Marcelo not only helped me get a better job by getting me fired, but he also helped my new dean get me a better apartment on campus than the one I had before, with free maid service twice a week and my own office in the house. I couldn't have asked for a better place to live. I also had a beautiful garden outside where I could relax after work.

Can bad people really hurt us? I don't think so. But it depends on how you look at the situation. For example, when my father kicked me out of the house, I was homeless, so to find a place to sleep, I would often go to coffee shops that were open 24 hours a day, or even libraries, and I would read there as an excuse to stay longer. I would fall asleep on the books and rest for at least three to four hours without anyone disturbing me. Thanks to my father, not only did I read more, but I also learned to sleep less, while at the same time learning how to find alternatives to sleeping on the streets. He let me develop my survival instinct. After that year,

I was never afraid of being homeless again, which also made me appreciate having a bed to sleep in.

This experience made me a resilient traveler, unafraid to explore the unknown. After traveling to several countries and not liking any of them, I just kept moving because I no longer needed any form of attachment.

After my mother kicked me out of the house because my stepfather didn't like me, accepting the unknown, even loneliness and darkness, became part of my nature. It was hard for a while to spend Christmas, my birthday and New Years alone, but after a few years I became insensitive to that as well.

Moreover, the suffering of loneliness made me develop ways to appreciate myself, which eventually led me to find ways to make myself happy, and that is how I became a writer.

Now I often meet people all over the world who think the opposite of me and cannot understand me. They ask me why I am always traveling, as if I have to stay somewhere, while in my mind the whole world belongs to me. I am not really traveling, I have just developed a broader concept of space compared to the average person who usually dies where he was born.

I remember being alone on a Greek island, with a beautiful view of the ocean, and thinking, my life is amazing, peaceful and beautiful, and all those who hate me are stuck in their own miserable realities. As I stroked the fur of the wild cat that visited me every day, I could only think that I wouldn't mind being dead, because I would be happy to be there too, as a ghost, experiencing the same.

The world has made me a ghost, and I have learned to enjoy it, but I have no pity for myself. On the contrary, I feel free and lucky to experience so much more than most people.

Chapter 2: Living the Dream Life

Should I be angry when my haters have led me to a life I could only dream of before?

According to surveys of the world's most popular jobs, being a writer tops the list, so it's only natural that I should be hated for living the life many secretly desire. According to a study by Remitly, the second most popular dream job based on global search volume for "how to be a..." is writer, followed by pilot (Remitly reports Q4 and full year 2022 results).

They could learn from me and read my books, but they don't because they have only hate in their hearts. They are often so arrogant that they think they can steal some secret from me to achieve the same thing.

Everyone asks, "How do you sell your books?" As if that is the secret to a successful life, because everyone is looking for a shortcut. People are lazy. They don't want an answer that involves hard work. No one has ever asked me how to write a book that is worth reading or that people want to buy, not even one person out of the thousands I have met over the years from all corners of the world.

For these reasons, I can't hate those who hate me, no matter how much they want to, because I pity them for their insignificance and absolute ignorance.

The problem with ignorant people is that no matter how many years go by, they insist on thinking they don't need to learn anything, and so they reach their 70s and think they're the wise wizard of Mount Olympus, talking nonsense.

I remember a conversation I had with a 70-year-old Rosicrucian that illustrates this perfectly when she said: "Everyone here agrees with me, so you must be wrong and arrogant to think you are right."

I looked at her and smiled, not even feeling offended. "Then you are all crazy," I said.

She stared at me in disbelief and horror and never spoke to me again.

She would not accept that I could correct her when she was talking a lot of nonsense, using words she didn't understand and applying them incorrectly. She thought she knew more about such words than I did, even though I had been an expert in learning disabilities for many years and had even helped students pass national psychology exams with high grades, which then allowed them to enter college and even compete with others who had taken classes in high school. I was also the president of the student union at the college and the spokesperson for student affairs, and that meant dealing mostly with students majoring in psychology, education, and literature.

This old lady was convinced that she knew more than me about the meaning of the words she used against me, all of which were related to psychology. It is like teaching a new martial art and then, after a few weeks of learning from you, another person who has never trained anything else in their life tries to beat you. Yes, this does happen. In fact, such students would get angry if none of their punches could hit me but mine hit them, as if throwing 20 bad punches is better than throwing one good punch filled with precision and efficiency.

People believe that a person with over 20 years of experience can be defeated by someone who has learned the same thing in a few weeks. People do not value training, hard work, or technique. They think it is enough to believe in their delusional self.

That old woman was the real arrogant one, but she was convinced that she was on the right track because many fools agreed with her foolishness. But what a misery. After that day I never felt the need to join another religious group. I am getting old because of so much foolishness and no more time to waste.

Over the years, I didn't get more sympathy and respect, but more insults from all religious groups, from both the oldest and the youngest people in such groups, which led me to conclude that they all follow psychopathic narratives and are drunk with their own delusions.

The most obvious thing to me, which no one seems to notice, is that all spiritual seekers suffer from learning disabilities or even mental disorders. They misinterpret texts, whether they were written years, decades, or thousands of years ago, and even misuse common words, leading others into confusion and illogical dogmas. I was glad to no longer be a part of that nonsense, but they also taught me the limitations of the average mind by their own actions and behaviors.

I had to read a lot to develop a metric system that showed me this, but it consisted of nothing more than asking real and simple questions. When I realized that most of the books people considered enlightening were extremely basic and simple, and that my own books already surpassed them in complexity and depth, I realized that being called arrogant, egotistical, and narcissistic was how people protected their fragile minds from the light of exposure of their absolute stupidity, inferiority, and jealousy. They felt small next to me and it made them uncomfortable.

Chapter 3: The Limits of Knowledge

I didn't expect Masons to feel small in my presence, but after talking to many of the most important Masons in the world, I realized that they, too, know too little. That's fine, but while you can pretend not to know, you can't hide strong emotions like jealousy. Most people fight over crumbs as they compete to see who knows more, who has more secrets, who has read the most relevant books.

I realized that I would be hated even more if I continued to be among them, and even more if I tried to help and teach them, so I continued my journey alone. I would eventually find a humble woman to keep me company, after spending many months with a wild cat for company. The cat taught me the value of resilience and patience, and that is enough for me. Simplicity bears the best fruit.

My best insights in life came when I was alone, facing the ocean. I learned to appreciate those moments of contemplation when there is only me, God and the sea. The best moments of my life were in Portugal, Greece and Albania. It would be better if I could replace their citizens with cats, but the fact that I could find moments of solitude and divine contemplation in such countries was good enough. It is always better than being alone on the beach in Spain and having the British stare at me all the time as if I were doing something illegal because I share the same ocean and sand with them. British people really disgust me at this point. I only close my eyes to those who read my books and trust no one else.

I've also been betrayed by all the British friends I've had before, which has led me to the conclusion that they can't be trusted. At least the Portuguese and the Spanish don't always try to betray you when you turn your back on them like the British do. It often seems that the British are so jealous that they plot our downfall from the moment they meet us. I had a British friend who once told me she wanted to help me sell more books and even set up a blog for me. I thought it was too good to be true, but since we knew each other for a long time, I let it happen as long as I had the password to such a blog. It didn't take me long to realize that she was taking phrases from my books out of context to make me look foolish. In essence, she was using Help as an excuse to put me down and make me fail.

When that strategy failed, she asked to edit the content of my books, and again I realized that she was deliberately altering them to make me look foolish. This time, when I told her that I could see what she was doing, she got angry, as if I was the ungrateful one.

Evil people love to make you feel guilty for what they do to you, as a way of nullifying their responsibility while downgrading your need to protect your integrity.

It is ironic that she wanted to write a book and was never able to, and I wonder if I was helping her or just showing her how incompetent she was for not succeeding.

The stupid see the world as a competition to get more, a competition for limited resources. They are easily triggered by jealousy and live with a tremendous amount of resentment inside them that they try to pass on to others in the form of hatred, and you can't always see it because they can be jealous of anything and everything, whether it's your job, your possessions, your relationships and accomplishments, or even your smile and advice to them.

It is very difficult to try to help them because they distort your intentions, just as they lie about their own intentions when they try to help you. You are trying to help them and they are trying to destroy you. The two realities couldn't be more different.

I've met people who have actually said that I'm irritating because I'm always happy and making jokes. They believe the world is unfair and biased against them, which fuels their anger and aggression toward others they perceive as having an advantage over them. They are unable to respect the achievements of others as a result of hard work and can only feel sympathy for their suffering.

Many of my family members seemed kind to me when I was poor and struggling in life. When I changed my life, they became angry. But none of them ever helped me with anything. They were angry because they wanted me to stay the way I was or even die trying to be better. My miserable reality gave them a sense of peace in their hearts.

Many people who claim to be good Christians are actually content to see misery in others and become demons when other people improve their lives. They even claim a form of divinity in themselves by being incompetent and lazy. They think that God keeps them poor so that they can be virtuous. It is a very sick way of looking at life that comes to the surface in the form of jealousy and hatred of what others do with work and study. Then you know their real thoughts.

Chapter 4: The Dangers of Ignorance

What amazes me most about stupid people is not only that they cling to a belief that validates their laziness, but also that they despise books and the act of studying for self-improvement. They even laugh at those who read self-help books, as if such books were for the retarded.

Because they see life as a continuation of the same state of mind as they see their own world, they think it's foolish to try to change anything instead of accepting it as it is. They will never see their own situation as a result of their lack of intelligence, their lack of empathy, and their limited view of life, but rather as a competition in which they are behind someone else whom they must defeat in order to move forward.

They have such hatred, fueled by their jealousy, that they secretly wish to kill those they envy, and they often try to do just that, either by creating conflict through slander, or by literally implying things about people that can get them arrested and killed. There is pure hate in their hearts.

Stupid people only refrain from violence when they fear negative consequences, although they usually provoke in front of others to make it look like you are crazy for reacting to them. They may even avoid physical violence if others are watching or if there is a possibility of being caught by the law, unless they are sure that those watching can help them.

This is especially true when a woman provokes a man in front of others. If she thinks she can get away with it, she will not hesitate to use violence as a means to achieve her ends. But because we live in a world full of idiots, people laugh when they see a woman attacking a man, and even watch as if it's entertaining, but condemn the man who responds, as if she didn't deserve a slap in the face.

Many adults in our world were not punished enough as children, so they grow up to be very childish adults, constantly provoking other people. This lack of education has its effects in adulthood, and now the entire society is responsible for dealing with such idiots.

It gets worse when society refuses to take responsibility for its own members. Then the only thing left is prison. Until then, there will be many victims along the way, and if none of them are killed, society will just continue to tolerate such idiots.

They may even lose all their jobs because of the constant abuse they inflict on others, and they will just go on living, moving from job to job and city to city, telling others how great they are and how selfless their actions were.

It is no coincidence that such women either become very fat, or if their bodies are too small to bully others and threaten them with physical violence, they will seek to marry a tall and fat man for protection, knowing that the more abusive she is, the more protection she will need.

Notice that the most abusive women always have strong men for husbands. Notice also that when these men are too kind, they are discarded and replaced by another who, like a pit bull trained to attack, will lash out at anyone she points her finger at.

When it comes to insults, fools often use them as a way to manipulate others and gain an advantage, and they know that by insulting someone in front of others, they can make that person look bad and themselves look good. This way they can gain the support and protection of the group while making themselves look like the victim, which gives credibility to their lies and tricks.

They also insult people when they think others are not listening, so they can make the person feel bad without facing any consequences. But interestingly, stupid people are very calculated in their insults. They insult others in a way that makes them think that the person being insulted is the crazy one. This allows them to gain sympathy from others and makes it easier for them to continue abusing their victims.

They can do this so convincingly that the victim himself begins to believe that he is the problem.

This is a common technique used by stupid people to manipulate and control others, but by understanding the psychology of stupid people, you can avoid becoming a victim of their abuse and in turn help others who may be in a similar situation.

You need to remember that most of their actions are triggered by childish jealousy, often over things you haven't even considered, such as traumas they have repressed in their own minds that, although irrelevant in adulthood, still trigger their core insecurities, such as feeling inadequate, insufficient, ugly, and unqualified.

Chapter 5: The Price of Excellence

In one of my jobs, I noticed that the director of the facility changed her feelings toward me from loving my work to hating me, and I couldn't understand why. The kids were happy, I had solved their learning disability problems, everyone's grades were going up, and everything was just positive, so why would she hate me? Well, the reason was that I was getting amazing results, or in other words, jealousy!

She was jealous that I was getting the results she never got and that the kids loved me and saw her as useless and annoying. She didn't care that I was making her rich, that I was helping her triple the income of the facility.

These kids were marketing the facility for free and bringing in more kids, their own friends, but jealousy really took precedence over her profits and even over the kids' results or their need for my support.

This is exactly how a stupid person thinks! She is so blinded by hate that she can destroy everything on her way to get the fame she is obsessed with.

I also found out years later that she divorced her husband, which is not surprising since she had gotten everything she wanted from him by that time.

Idiots have a utilitarian view of life, and as much as they are jealous, competitive, and in need of social satisfaction and admiration, which means they will destroy anything and anyone in their way to get what they want.

If the only thing standing in their way is a divorce, they will take advantage of that too, and then replace the previous partner with a new one, as if they were shopping for new toys, because they also see others as a means to their ends.

One of my former girlfriends decided to cheat on me with a man who convinced her that he could help her get her own opportunity on a local television station with her own show. I knew this was a lie, and it became obvious when she told me this that she was either cheating or planning to cheat because she was too excited about the idea to let it go. But the stupid fool the stupid, and the stupid are so obsessed with their delusions that not only can they easily manipulate each other, but they have no way of knowing when someone is fooling them the way they fool others.

Months later, when she realized her mistake, she tried to get back into my life, which was obviously impossible, but fools also have a poor sense of reality and no accountability for their actions, so she sent me letters every month telling me how much she loved me.

The average person has no perception of these half-humans among us, so they really believe that such individuals can love. They can't, and they don't even know what love is. For them, love is what they see in movies, because they learn by imitation.

How do I know this? She told me herself.

Eventually they become experts at using the same words and phrases they see in the movies to convince another person that there is love between them, but for them love is really just whatever you perceive it to be.

I once had a conversation with my female students about this because I wanted to know how easily they could be fooled, and they said that love is when they feel good, so I asked them if giving them the things they want would make them fall in love with someone, and they all said yes.

"Then you are all easily deceived," I said. But they took that as an insult.

People are so determined to believe that they know everything and that what they see in movies is the ultimate truth, without considering who is behind the movie scripts and with what intent, or how successful or unsuccessful those individuals are in their own lives, that they take it for granted and assume that they can learn everything they need from movies.

They remind me of dogs running after balls they see thrown on a television screen. Fools really are that easily fooled into believing what they see. They have no capacity for reason or critical thinking.

When you try to educate them and raise them to a higher level of ability to analyze reality, they get offended as if you are taking away the only thing they know about life and turning them into lost and negative creatures.

I have often been accused of being too negative in teaching others how to think, as if not knowing how the world works and trusting in fantasy is much better. The phrase "ignorance is bliss" was obviously spread by a fool and has credibility only among fools.

Chapter 6: Bullying as a Symptom of Fear

Stupid people tend to live in constant fear of the world around them because they do not understand it. They need to measure the effect of their insults and threats, which gives them a sense of power over others. Power, in turn, makes them feel safe and in control of their reality.

Whenever you take that power away from them, they feel insecure and immediately start spreading smear campaigns to bring you down and remove you from a social circle.

One reason they may do this publicly is that they believe that if they are seen bullying someone else, they will be perceived as strong, even if their target is weaker or simply not interested in fighting back.

They may pick on the same target to continue to get their boost of validation and project a false sense of entitlement and strength.

Although this is easy to observe with children, in the office, or in a relationship, this bullying takes the form of what we know as invalidation. "You are not good enough" is the typical phrase either said or implied in the dynamic.

Over time, the psychological abuse affects the victim's thought patterns, lowering their self-confidence and making them more apologetic and conforming to the norm.

This is called a self-fulfilling prophecy, as the victim begins to act and think as they are expected to think and act based on the smear campaigns and treatment they have received.

Not surprisingly, children raised by narcissistic parents may begin to act helpless and even retarded because they feel safer that way.

Over the years, they internalize that appearing smart, confident, and proactive triggers their parents' vulnerability and launches their attacks on them, often in the form of insults and threats.

My mother used to yell at me when she saw me reading books and would even find excuses to stop me, like telling me to go buy groceries. When that didn't work, she would unleash her insults, calling me crazy, abnormal, and other nasty names.

My father did the same thing, often calling me stupid for refusing to go along with his lies.

This is how such people react when their power is threatened, and especially when they see you evolving in life.

Over the years, I saw the exact same reactions in my sister and many other family members, which forced me to realize that I was not dealing with people, but beasts, demons in human flesh.

It is impossible to communicate with such people or to make them understand reason and common sense. They can only pretend to agree with you in order to gain time to further invalidate you and find more information about you that they can later use to destroy you more effectively.

It is truly impossible to be around such individuals because you can see it in their eyes, they are demonically possessed, they can't control themselves and stop, they are obsessed with your own destruction.

They constantly trick you into relaxing, lowering your guard, and just letting them get through with their psychological warfare. They will even tell you so themselves:

- "Why are you always so nervous and can't relax?"

"Why are you so suspicious of me and don't believe anything I say?"

"I can't talk to you if you don't believe me!"

"I love you and this is for your own good."

Saying "I'm doing this because I love you" is actually the narcissist's favorite phrase because it spreads confusion through aggression.

This is why many victims of narcissistic abuse end up confusing love with psychological abuse.

As we grow apart from these interactions, we may not even realize that we are constantly avoiding conflict with toxic personalities, which actually attracts them more because they see it as weakness. It is as if narcissists can smell the effect of other narcissists on you, as if they are all working together in the same narrative to make you weaker and more vulnerable over time.

No narcissist ever hurts you enough on his own, unless you compare his actions to those of the previous ones.

The victims of stupid people then end up acting like they have no self-worth, which in turn affects their results in life and even how they are perceived by other people.

This is because the victims have internalized traits that are not threatening to narcissistic family members: Not being confident, not having or showing talents or skills, not thinking, not judging or observing factually, not being pragmatic or effective, not questioning the validity of what is heard, not contesting, and most importantly, not resisting the abuse.

Victims of abusive parents not only attract abusive partners, but often stay with them for years before they realize they have been tricked into accepting a worthless person and even developing feelings for such a person.

It takes time for someone to realize their mistakes, and of course this does not happen without self-therapy, or at least cultivating the qualities the narcissists tried to keep you from having: Consciousness, self-love, self-awareness, self-care, and critical thinking.

Chapter 7: Rising Above Fear

Most people have no critical thinking whatsoever and simply repeat what they see others do because society is dominated by either narcissists or narcissist enablers - people who have learned to be helpless and to obey without question, often because they are paid to do so.

Narcissists know that if your survival depends on your decisions, they can keep your salary low enough and your bank account minimal enough that you won't have a chance on your own once you are financially punished.

Besides, what do narcissists and their enablers keep telling you? Money is not important.

Why do they say that? Because if you believe it, you are always easier to manipulate.

Who do they hate the most? The rich and the free, because they can't be persuaded by lies.

There's nothing they hate more than the fact that I can leave their country anytime I want, and I don't need them for anything, not for validation, not for comfort, not for friendship. This really makes them angry.

How do they try to belittle me? They can't say money isn't important because that clearly doesn't work with me. Instead, they use sex and loneliness as weapons against me. They say I need to get married and that it's easier if I live somewhere permanent. They also say I need to put down roots and that traveling around the world will make me lonely.

These things have no correlation, but they find the correlations for you to stop you and control you and bring you down to their level because they are jealous of what you have.

They all want these things for themselves. If you fail in life, even that will be used against you.

It is also not uncommon for narcissists to use religion as an extension of their own coercion. They often claim "you're not doing what God wants" or "you're not following the Bible," even though they don't quote anything from the Bible to justify their accusations, and they use God in their sentences as if they were some special messenger from Him.

Worse than that is when a narcissist is the only one who can read Latin and all the Bibles are written in Latin. Christians used to burn people alive for translating the Bible for this reason, because then you can't lie to such people, because only the clergy were educated in Latin.

The Tyndale Bible, translated by William Tyndale in the 16th century, was the first English Bible to draw directly from Hebrew and Greek texts, and it was also the first English Bible to take advantage of the printing press for wide distribution, but Tyndale paid the price with his own life. He was burned at the stake in 1536.

Today, the solution to the falsehoods being spread lies in the distance of a common dictionary that people don't even use because they assume they know the meanings of the words they hear told to them by those in power. But people have no concept of the vast majority of words they use on a daily basis. This is why they are so easily manipulated into following nonsense.

The dumber someone is, the easier it is to get them to do anything. For example, people who blindly use the word science to force others to do something are doing the exact opposite of what the word science implies. From the Latin word scientia, a derivative of the Latin verb "scire," science means to know. Doing science is the act of studying or acquiring knowledge. If you refuse to discuss science, you are not doing science, you are using dogma, just like a religion.

Science is now being used as a religion to trick the average fool into obeying without questioning or thinking for himself. Also, just as the Latin Bibles could only be interpreted by the clergy, the average person does not have access to the meanings of most of the words used by scientists and is therefore a functional illiterate when it comes to interpreting the ingredients in the food he buys at any supermarket.

When the abusers succeed in making you fail, they also seem to want to save you, which is why the same people who use science to destroy your health seem to have the cure for you. And isn't it amazing how the same companies sell you the drugs with side effects and more drugs to treat the same side effects with different side effects?

The wicked of the world always seem to want to pull you up after they have deceived you and while they are looking for a cliff to throw you over again. They will then use your failures to further assert their superiority, as when a mother tricks her daughter into believing that her boyfriend can leave her, which then leads the daughter to test the validity of such a claim. When the boyfriend finally succumbs to the emotional abuse, packs up and leaves, the mother is waiting with open arms and a warm smile.

As they embrace again, the mother says in a victorious tone, "I told you so. But all along, the mother never wanted her daughter to be with a man who would not give the mother money and would use her daughter as a transactional object.

This is exactly what one narcissistic mother told me when she kept saying, "This is the only daughter I have.

Why should she worry about having only one daughter? Because only daughters can be exchanged for money, they are the most commonly exchanged commodity in poor countries.

Narcissistic parents always see the relationship between their sons and daughters as a transaction, which is why my mother would get angry when girls would call me if such girls were not from rich families.

Chapter 8: The Cost of Ignorance in Health Care

Manipulation isn't the only negative side of being around narcissists, because they'd rather have you sick and in bed than free to do whatever you want.

Not only are there morons who are afraid of being perceived as useless, they would rather have everyone around them sick, dying, and helpless because it makes them feel safer.

It may be hard to believe, but it is very common to see a psychologist, psychiatrist, or doctor smile when he sees one of his patients come back with the same problem he had when they first met. Noticing this strengthens the bond between a narcissist and his patients more than having them come to the same clinic for many years. They are even proud of it. But don't you find it strange when a clinic has the same patient for decades?

I used to go to the same dentist for many years, even when I lived in different countries, simply because I trusted her. She would not find excuses to make money from me like the others, or so

I thought. That was before I discovered what she never told me: What I was eating was changing the health of my teeth.

Dentists will never tell you this and will instead convince you to use fluoride toothpaste with a much higher risk of poisoning, toothpaste so toxic it affects your brain. They make more money prescribing toothpaste while claiming to be helping you.

The real reason comes out when you refuse to pay more for their toothpaste because they get angry. That was when I realized I was not going back to that clinic. Instead, I looked for the cures they told me did not exist, and I found them. Since then, I have not had a single problem with my teeth.

They tell you that health problems are genetic, so you give up looking for solutions, and what I found is that all health problems come from a mineral deficiency, which by the way is very common in people, precisely because nobody tells them.

The world is kept in the dark with lies so that many can profit from such lies. It's a vicious cycle that people perpetuate to make money out of other people's ignorance, as if they were planting fruit on their brains. The more shit you have in your head, the more fertilizer their tree of greed gets and the more profit they make.

Interestingly, the most important minerals are also kept hidden, expensive or hard to find. They even tell you that some of them are bad for you, like iodine in salt. Others are magnesium, zinc, iron, and selenium.

They also tell you that caffeine is great to keep you energized, when the truth is that coffee interferes with mineral absorption, causing a more pronounced mineral deficiency, which then leads to a lack of calcium, especially in the bones.

They lie when they tell you that you need laser teeth cleaning every 3 months because they can profit from it. They will never tell you that the need for such a deep cleaning is caused by demineralization and that you can save your money by changing your diet to include more vitamin K, that is, simply by adding broccoli, kale, sprouts, parsley, asparagus and spinach to your diet.

I have met dozens of doctors in my life, in different countries, including China, India, Thailand, Spain and Lithuania, and not one of them has said this. Nor has any doctor said that coffee is a diuretic, which means that it increases urine production, resulting in the loss of water-soluble vitamins and minerals, such as potassium and magnesium, through increased urination.

Since we live in a world of liars and fools, what you see most is death being promoted everywhere, and what you see least is health.

Then those in control tell you that everything is normal and that you are a conspiracy theorist for asking too many questions and doubting the usual narratives.

A dentist I met in Malaysia was shocked when I told her that the Nazis used fluoride to keep prisoners in concentration camps docile, and that fluoride or similar components are the main ingredient in various antidepressants.

She didn't seem interested in debunking me. Instead, she kept repeating that she had been told in college that fluoride was good for the teeth, as if she were nothing more than a circus monkey who would repeat whatever she was told.

Most people in the world are like this woman, which is why you are forbidden to even access information on the subject when you research it, and then ridiculed for discussing it with others.

Chapter 9: The Silent Threat to Cognitive Health

Stupidity has many causes, but fluoride is certainly one of them. Although experts may claim that fluoride and fluorine are not the same and that only fluorine is used in antidepressants, steroids, and anesthetics, you should know that several studies have documented elevated levels of fluoride in the urine or blood after use of these drugs, challenging the notion that organofluorine compounds are metabolically inert.

For example, fluorinated anesthetics such as sevoflurane have been shown to increase serum and urine fluoride levels. Mazze et al (1992) investigated the fluoride toxicity of sevoflurane anesthesia and found that prolonged exposure to sevoflurane may result in fluoride toxicity. The authors stated, "Sevoflurane is metabolized to release fluoride ions, which may result in elevated serum fluoride levels. Prolonged exposure to sevoflurane may result in fluoride toxicity.

Fluorinated steroids, such as fluticasone propionate, have also been studied for their potential to release fluoride ions during metabolism. Derendorf et al (1995) studied the fluoride metabolism of fluticasone propionate and found that metabolism of this drug results in increased urinary fluoride levels. The authors reported, "Fluticasone propionate, a fluorinated steroid, is metabolized to release fluoride ions that can be detected in the urine. This results in increased urinary fluoride levels."

Meanwhile, we are witnessing the increasing prevalence of organofluorinated compounds in modern drug formulations because they improve the metabolic stability, increase the lipophilicity and modify the bioavailability of drugs, which are critical factors in drug design and development.

Both fluoride and fluorine are highly toxic to humans and other organisms, yet they are found in anti-inflammatory drugs, antibiotics, and even common beverages such as wine and soda. Fluoride has also been found in sodium fluoroacetate, also known as Compound 1080 and more commonly known as rat poison, since the 1800s. It is also found in insecticides, pesticides and herbicides used in agriculture.

Bayer played a significant role in the Nazi war effort by producing Zyklon B, a pesticide later used in the gas chambers of Nazi death camps. The company also used forced labor from concentration camps during World War II. Today, Bayer is responsible for producing a wide range of products containing fluorine-based compounds, from antidepressants (such as Prozac and Paxil) to anesthetics and pesticides, as well as fluoride toothpaste, fluoride supplements, and fluorinated polymers used in non-stick cookware and waterproof clothing.

Fluoride has been found to have the same brain-damaging effects as lead, mercury, arsenic, PCBs, and toluene. In addition to acting as a neurotoxin that can cause brain disorders such as autism and ADHD, it has also been shown to reduce intelligence, impair the ability to learn and remember, and increase the likelihood of developing Alzheimer's disease.

Choi and colleagues (2012) examined the link between fluoride exposure and neurodevelopment in children, and found that children in high-fluoride areas had significantly lower IQ scores than those in low-fluoride areas.

Fluoride has also been linked to attention deficit hyperactivity disorder (ADHD). A study by Till et al (2015) examined the association between exposure to fluoridated water and the prevalence of ADHD in the United States, and found that states with higher proportions of people receiving fluoridated water from public water systems tended to have higher proportions of children and adolescents diagnosed with ADHD. Guan et al (1998) found that fluoride may affect brain cell metabolism and nervous system development.

The possible role of fluoride in the pathogenesis of Alzheimer's disease has also been investigated in the scientific literature. Luke (2001) examined the relationship between fluoride and Alzheimer's disease and found that fluoride readily crosses the blood-brain barrier and accumulates in the brain, particularly in the pineal gland and hippocampus, areas implicated in the onset of Alzheimer's disease. This accumulation of fluoride in the brain may also contribute to the development of other neurodegenerative diseases.

Over the years fluoride has been identified in various studies as a neurotoxin with potential adverse effects on intelligence, learning and memory, but people are being deliberately dumbed down and deliberately kept stupid, and the more they avoid talking about it or seeing the problem for what it is, a problem of mass stupidity, the more likely it is to continue because nobody is going to do anything about it.

There's nothing dumber than ignoring this information.

Chapter 10: The Neurotoxic Effects of Fluoride

Fluoride's effect on cognitive function is due to several mechanisms:

First, fluoride has been shown to interfere with the activities of brain enzymes. Enzymes are critical to various biochemical pathways in the brain, and their disruption can lead to altered neuronal function and neurodevelopmental outcomes.

Second, fluoride exposure has been linked to oxidative stress, a condition in which there is an imbalance between free radicals and antioxidants in the body. Oxidative stress can damage brain cells and has been implicated in several neurodegenerative diseases and cognitive impairments.

Another important aspect of fluoride's effect on brain function is its interaction with the thyroid gland. The thyroid plays a critical role in brain development, especially in the early stages of life. It secretes hormones that regulate metabolism, growth, and brain development. Fluoride exposure has been linked to changes in thyroid function that could affect children's neurodevelopment and cognitive abilities.

We now live in a world with a large number of incredibly stupid people due to this massive poisoning, among many other factors that accentuate the manifestation of ignorance. With so many people ingesting soda, antidepressants, and antibiotics, is it any wonder that there is such a pandemic of stupidity in the world?

There seems to be a correlation between depression and stupidity, not only because fluoride exposure leads to depression, but also because antidepressants increase stupidity. Side effects of fluoride-containing medications include impaired concentration, learning, and memory, as well as mental symptoms such as anxiety, tension, and depression. Prolonged exposure to fluoride also leads to hypothyroidism, which causes symptoms such as fatigue and weight gain.

If any of this sounds familiar, it is because you have been duped into normalizing the ingestion of poison into your body with the argument that it is good for you because everyone is doing it and health experts recommend it.

Although it is not stupid to not know that there are many people who profit from mass ignorance for their financial gain, it is stupid to think that this is the only way to live in this world. But everyone is taught in school that everything is a competition to get the most popularity and money. In fact, it is not surprising that medical and psychology students hide papers that teachers have left out for everyone to read, believing that they are competing for the best grades.

Few of them understand that this simply forces the teacher to print more papers, repeat the exam, and invalidate the previous exam, wasting everyone's time. Even fewer realize the implications of living in a world where they have to interact with people no one is really helping.

Altruism is not something that interests many in the health care industry. It is the same when we are all being poisoned because no one cares enough about others to do anything about it.

Stupid people are too obsessed with themselves to think about the consequences of their actions, which is why they sometimes get beaten up for being rude or die in very stupid ways.

No one cares if the stupid get drunk and crash into a wall, but they often take innocent lives along the way, so you always have to be careful in a world of stupid people.

Where do people often die? Crossing the street on a green light.

In the United States, more people die each year as pedestrians than as victims of muggings. According to the FBI, there are about 1,200 robbery homicides in the United States each year, but the National Highway Traffic Safety Administration (NHTSA) shows us that there are 6,000 pedestrian deaths each year.

What is the lesson here? Following the rules when an idiot is around is more deadly than being the idiot or being targeted by an idiot.

Chapter 11: Exposing the Fraud in Education

When it comes to the education system, and based on what I've seen, stupid teachers are proud of the number of students they can fail.

Since Portugal is basically a country with a vast majority of stupid people, as we have verified based on the data of the coronavirus pandemic of 2019 and the fact that the entire population was duped into voluntarily injecting a poison into their bodies without knowing the negative long-term effects, many teachers in this country are extremely happy when they can fail everyone in their exams.

Not surprisingly, these same college professors get their own bachelor's and master's degrees in other countries, especially countries where professors don't fail their students no matter how stupid they are, namely post-Soviet countries and communist countries in general.

The rudest, most arrogant, and most incompetent teachers I had in college all, without exception, got their college degrees abroad, in universities that don't fail students, and then started teaching without any significant work experience. They used the family money as leverage, and because they were too incompetent, they had to show their arrogance by belittling others, especially students like me, whom they hated for no other reason than to challenge their false authority.

Not surprisingly, they were all socialists and communists, because those are the political systems that favor the arrogant and the stupid, not the most competent among us, for another common characteristic of the stupid is their hypocrisy.

The more effort someone makes to appear intelligent, the more likely it is that their background shows the opposite. But when a stupid person is identified as such, their fear goes to another level and their threats become more intense because they feel trapped.

I have never been attacked as much as when I have consulted for the military. It is like spraying poison in an old house full of cockroaches. There is so much corruption, money laundering and theft going on that they will do their best to get me out if I get too close to the truth.

Institutions filled with stupid people only accept being investigated on the premise that the investigator will not reveal the truth about them. That's the illusion the stupid live in!

No university wants students who are smart enough to ask the questions that make their teachers look stupid, or worse, cheaters, and that's what I often found in my research. But in the same way, no famous institution wants to be exposed as incompetent and especially as using taxpayers' money for money laundering.

People will not only slander you and fire you, they will try to ruin your life and make you disappear, as they did to me, for no other reason than to conduct a normal investigation to know why so much money was invested in the military and the money kept disappearing.

That is why you cannot trust any institution, especially in this case, because my professors were involved in the fraud.

Eventually the government catches on to these things, and as long as its members do not have their hands in the cookie jar, they will see the obvious. It can take many years, and rarely, if ever, does anyone go to jail when it happens.

Since the stupid tend to create a vast network of people who will do them favors and bulldoze anything in their way that doesn't favor them, their fear comes precisely from having their plans exposed by someone else. This can include losing their jobs, going to jail, being beaten, or even killed, depending on the situation.

Stupid people are so afraid of being found out and destroyed that they rarely reveal where they live, work, or socialize.

One of the reasons for this fear is that they know that if smart people were to find them, they would be exposed and vulnerable. Dumb people are often aware of their limitations and feel that they are no match for smart people, so they use their bullying tactics to intimidate others and try to avoid exposing themselves to potential threats.

Dumb people are perceived as bullies, but they are actually weak, so they often go into hiding to protect themselves. This behavior is driven by their fear of confrontation and death.

They know that if they are exposed, they can be easily defeated, so they seek refuge from others. In a way, they like to bully in front of others to be seen as strong, but when their target reacts, they get scared and may disappear completely.

For the same reasons, they are constantly afraid of being exposed, which is why they are afraid of others discovering their social media accounts, Internet browsing history, and even their travel plans.

This fear is rooted in their belief that exposing their personal information can lead to vulnerability and potential harm. If and when they do share their personal lives, they will only share useless images or images that give them some validation, such as a photo of themselves and their family.

Chapter 12: Dealing with Provocation

It is not uncommon for stupid people to attack intelligent people for the very reasons that make them afraid of being exposed as liars and manipulators, so the intelligent person may have absolutely no reason to respond with violence until he is systematically provoked by someone who is simply scared. These provocations are triggered by their own insecurities.

If I meet a 74-year-old writer who can barely walk and he keeps insulting me, there is only one reason: He feels insecure and like a loser because I have more results than he does.

He doesn't realize that my results are due to my quality as a writer, because he's too stupid to see that. Instead, he is convinced that insulting me will make him feel better. And what am I supposed to do? Slap him in the face?

Stupid people don't realize how pathetic their behavior is, and they can act that way until they die. The best way to deal with them is to let them die as the miserable creatures they are and always have been.

I think I have never attracted as much hate as I have since I became a full-time writer, because nothing scares stupid people more than having to deal with someone who produces knowledge for others, who gives them eyes to see.

Intelligent people love writers, stupid people hate them, but secretly want to become one in order to influence public opinion. When they are desperate for attention, the stupid write books, which is why there is so much useless literature in the world, but they obviously do it to spread confusion in the world while gaining more credibility for themselves.

The most useless books I have read in my life have all been written by college professors who are desperate for credibility without any reason to deserve it. They disguise their stupidity by using complex words and filling their arguments with points of view that make you wonder if you are in a maze trying to get anywhere or just running away from the same chaos their vocabulary creates in your brain.

Who is the person they hate the most? The one who writes objectively.

Meanwhile, they will go through his writing trying to understand what can be copied to get the same results while deceiving the readers.

This is exactly what everyone who envied me tried to do when they read my works.

When I was younger, I thought I could find some common ground for peace, but the more you deal with stupid people, the more frustrated you get, and eventually you come to the conclusion that you can't get peace from them because they want you dead, literally dead.

My mother used to tell me stories about people who committed suicide, probably most of them made up, just to give me all the options to end my life. At the same time, she wanted me to believe that my life was useless and that I was doomed to be a failure, because you can't play with just one card, you have to play many cards to win this demonic game.

My father used to tell me that I had to pay for my own college because he could not afford it, and then he would steal my money and buy things for himself and the women he was dating. At the same time, he would insist that I was too stupid to understand life, as if he were wiser, while he robbed me and worked all his life at a job someone else offered him, never having to make any significant effort for anything in his life except to exist, which apparently was too difficult for him as well.

I thanked him for saying I was dead to him and that he would never apologize for what he did, especially for making me homeless because I then traveled east instead of west and invested my money in my future instead of going back to solve the problems I didn't create in my past.

I don't care about the lies a narcissist insists on telling everyone, nor do I expect pigs to fly and people to face reality as it is and not as they are told. I have gotten more out of life by moving on instead of trying to fix the stupid. I always find more when I am alone and much faster.

Great people also show up along the way. Some of the most interesting conversations I have had have been with business owners I never expected to meet, often when I visited their store, restaurant or coffee shop. Even the apartments I rented on my travels were often owned by successful business owners, which allowed me to have many interesting and enriching conversations.

Chapter 13: Childish Games of Stupidity

It is not that poor people are necessarily stupid while rich people are smarter, but that is often the case. It is rare to find an intelligent person without money, just as it is hard to find a rich person who is too stupid. So it happens that if you are a curious person who is interested in learning, you often find yourself talking to another curious person who is interested in learning. Both teach each other.

The rich learn from me as much as I learn from them. The poor and stupid insult and assume that they already know everything and that the rest are just secrets that they have to copy or steal.

Meanwhile, the greatest secret of the stupid is the stupidity they hide from themselves.

Stupid people have such a narrow view of life that they are unable to see other people as they really are, and they can only see the surface of reality, or less than that, because they are often filled with prejudice.

This means that their conversations are basically childish and rooted in a fantasy about life.

Not surprisingly, many of them are also addicted to video games, fantasy films, and Disney movies, because when reality seems too much for the brain, it can only find comfort in more fantasy. The less someone is able to face the reality of the world, the more they seek the comfort of their own fantasies. But they also find comfort in judging others rather than themselves for the same reasons: Their own reality is too negative.

The worse a person feels about himself, the more obsessed he becomes with judging others.

These are the ones who praise their co-workers for being pretty or condemn them for being ugly, judge them for being too fat or too thin, comment on what they wear, the type of partner they are with, and other very superficial things they can use to make themselves relevant while being completely irrelevant.

Judging others is how useless people find their place in the world. They think it makes them smarter. These are the same people you see on the street staring at others with arrogance and discriminating eyes.

In groups like the Jehovah's Witnesses, the level of childish conversation takes the form of their family, because they judge a person's character by how obedient they are to their own parents. It is also the easiest way to judge someone else, because an adult is likely to disagree with outdated views of life, especially if they have been around for 2,000 years.

Stupid people are childish, so it's not surprising that this religion is filled with retarded morons. You understand this when you realize that you can't argue with them about things they can't explain, or explain anything to them that contradicts the fantasies they want to believe in.

Like a child, they will run away from confrontation about their behavior and beliefs, even though they are constantly changing based on the dictates of those above them.

Another aspect you will find in common between stupid people and the religions they are attracted to is a lack of intellectual curiosity. They live in a small bubble and judge the world based only on their limited view of it. And the smaller their bubble, the more comfortable they are, as if they unconsciously want to return to their mother's womb.

That is why you see extremism, and not surprisingly, you see extremists playing childish games, like when the Taliban, after conquering Afghanistan in 2021, occupied merry-go-rounds meant for children and had their fun there. They literally killed for the right to play. You can't get more childish than that!

Of course, this form of childish behavior then takes on other forms that are less socially acceptable because, not surprisingly, childish men also tend to be pedophiles, and that's why the Taliban force marriages with underage girls.

You think the world's problems are related to terrorism, mass shooters, religion, the cruelty of tyrants, communism, and so on, but when you look deeper you realize that all these problems have in common human stupidity, or in other words, an absolute level of mental retardation.

We often don't see it as such, because then we have to answer another question, which is: "Why can the retards get so much power and influence?"

That leads us to the other side of the question that we don't want to face, which is ourselves. The reason morons get so much power is because everyone else allows it.

Of course, it's not an easy problem to solve, because when an idiot insults me, I don't know whether to slap him or insult him back, both responses seem childish, and yet these individuals leave you with no option but violence.

How do you respond when an adult acts like a child and traps you in his games? How do you apply the law when others don't see the problem for what it is, or worse, give authority to the childish man in power just because he works for the government, is a police officer, a security guard, or a doctor?

Stupid people just don't give you an alternative to socially unacceptable violence. In fact, they bet that you won't use it against them to perpetuate their abuse.

Chapter 14: The Puppeteers of Ignorance

Because most people are too stupid, they can't tell when one is acting more stupidly than the other. They lack the discernment and critical ability to do so because of years of indoctrination in a stupid system that has told them that questioning authority is bad.

You are essentially alone in dealing with these situations, and that means that people may not and will never understand why you stopped talking to a family member, or why you yelled at them and insulted them. They may use your reactions to the abuse against you to judge you even more negatively.

This means that the destruction caused by stupid people is indeed great, because you can't even react without removing the few pillars that were still standing. You will lose friends, family members, and maybe even your sons and daughters through divorce.

When the circus burns, the clown burns with it, and guess who is the clown in the circus of fools? It is you!

You are the one they have gone to great lengths to make everyone believe is the fool. They've done it so carefully, for so long, that by the time you realize the result, it's too late.

People don't want to change their minds about you because it makes them look stupid, even though the beliefs they've accumulated through deception are the very thing that makes them stupid.

They have no discernment, they can't tell the difference. The dumber someone is, the easier they are to manipulate, which doesn't mean that a smart person can't be manipulated.

The stupid person manipulates the dumb person by distorting facts, and the smart person by controlling emotions. If the stupid person being manipulated is the mother of the smart person, then the stupid person can accomplish two goals with only one strategy.

In an institution, the stupid person will gain control of the most powerful leader, which is what one of my colleagues did when she told him that all the work I did was done by her and that I was merely her assistant. Would this man realize that he had been deceived for two years? Absolutely not! He lashed out at me when I decided to quit!

He was too stupid to be my boss, so he was forced to close the doors when I left. But he did make me wonder how so many stupid people could be rich.

I guess that question answers itself, because he has employers like me and business partners and even a father who made him think he could hide his own stupidity behind other people's accomplishments and intellect.

Stupid people are stupid, so they can't analyze beyond their immediate observations; they judge others by their posture, facial expressions, and body language. They are more likely to be fooled and less likely to admit failure or change their point of view, so they make more mistakes than a normal person, and often in stupid ways, like believing everything they are told.

They may even invest in this kind of knowledge, seeing it as a better guarantee for manipulating others. It's not uncommon for stupid people to join drama groups and read extensively about body language and mind control books for this very reason.

I knew someone who was a narcissist who was obsessed with spy books and books on hypnosis and mind control. She would read anything she could find on these subjects because her mind revolved around them.

She did not believe in real friendships. Her first words when she came home after spending the day with a group of friends were: "I hate those people!" and then she would scream even louder while grabbing her head, "I hate them! I hate them! I hate them!"

She was considered very smart and kind by everyone, because the stupid are actually experts at making themselves look smart. They do this by actually studying what makes other people perceive someone as smart.

If you watch a group of stupid people talking, you can see how they do it. They will often mention a source that no one can find, or a book that doesn't exist, or explain that they met someone who gave them the information.

There's always a story that can't be proven to make themselves look smart. But then you look at their words and they are often full of conspiracies and no real information, nothing to learn, nothing useful. It's all just balloons of hot air to make themselves look special.

It is even more interesting when you find out that the stupidest person in the group stole your stupid girlfriend who always caused fights for the stupidest reasons and she dumped you to be with him.

In that case, when I found out, I couldn't be angry because I didn't feel like I lost anything of value or that she gained anything better. That's the thing about stupid people, they are so bad at making choices that they can surprise you with their stupidity and betrayal, often making a much worse choice when they cheat with someone else. It is as if they are helping you when they think they are doing the opposite.

Chapter 15: Dealing with Narcissists

It is really hard to get angry about what narcissists do. It is like finding out that your dog has been hiding bones in the corners of the house. It doesn't really matter. The people they cheat with say much more about them than they do about us. They free us to make better choices when they leave our lives.

Marcelo, the man who went to great lengths to get me fired from my teaching job, is still working as a teacher. He will probably die a teacher. He spends his days thinking about how to make himself look smarter so that no one will think he is stupid, so his mind is obsessed with his fears. Meanwhile, I have traveled the world and enjoyed my life. Could I be angry with Marcelo?

He accelerated my decisions when I needed to find a better job in a better university, he made me find smarter students and smarter colleagues, which in turn made me a better and faster writer. It is as if the harder they try to downgrade our reputations and destroy our lives, the better they make everything.

I could say the same thing about my parents. They were so psychologically abusive that they turned me into an intellectual machine, probably the most prolific writer in human history, for no other reason than a thirst for knowledge. Could I be angry with them?

They've never visited more than three or four countries in their lives, and they're stuck in a job they hate and the routine of spending every day with people they don't like, while I can wake up when I want, go where I want, and do what I want with my time. I can even spend a whole month making music when I don't feel like writing. Should I hate them?

Maybe their goal was to make me commit suicide, and in a way they succeeded, I stopped being who I was and became someone else. But is this new person the real one or the fake one?

It's a difficult question, but not impossible to answer. You are always the best version of yourself, so when others try to diminish you and stop you, they have made you better against their will, and maybe against your own.

Eventually they won't even recognize you, because stupid people tend to stay in the same place mentally. They don't listen, and they have little capacity to absorb new information. Instead, they create an imaginary idealization of the person in front of them and then accept only the audio or visual information that correlates with the image they have formed in their mind.

The foolish people who have met me can only accept the image they have formed in their minds and will never be able to see the person I have become. That is why Christ said (in Matthew 8:22), "Let the dead bury their dead.

On the other hand, the limited ability to perceive reality means that stupid people are often xenophobic and racist. Their racism works like this: "If someone is brown, he is poor, so I am rich and smarter because my skin is white. If the brown person is a writer or rich, he's doing something illegal and is a liar, because reality can't be what others think it is, and I'm always right and can't be wrong. If I am wrong, I am crazy, but I am perfect, so others must be hiding the truth.

This distorted view of reality is born out of their limitations, so the more stupid someone is, the more assumptions and judgments they make about the world.

That's why when a stupid cashier in Croatia doesn't know how to operate the card reader, she says to the brown person trying to pay: "There's no money in the card!"

She could say anything, like "It doesn't work!" but that's when you know someone is a racist and a stupid idiot.

After some time of hearing so many of these stupid phrases, you get tired of living in a certain country, which is why I think Croatia is a shithole filled with cockroaches that should have disappeared like so many other nations that were wiped out by other countries.

Another form of discrimination is when you stand in line to pay for your groceries and notice that the Albanian cashier says "Thank you! Have a nice day" to the Dutch woman with white skin in front of you, but says nothing to you because your skin is brown, which is why Albania is another shithole that was not a victim of wars, but rather a victim of the stupidity of its own people.

In the minds of the stupid, these behaviors are completely normal, so if you get angry, it's your problem, never theirs. When they start a war, they are always the victims, never the aggressors.

They see you as the crazy one because you are not acting out the roles that are preconceived for you based on the stupidity in their heads.

That's why when I walked into a coffee shop in Krakow, Poland, wearing a suit, the owner stared at me as if my suit offended him. He looked me up and down, even at my shoes, like a little bitch. But could I be angry about the situation when I decided to stay in this neo-Nazi nation?

I already knew that Poland was one of the biggest shitholes in the world. I just didn't know how bad it stunk.

Chapter 16: Confronting the Darkness in Society

There's always some truth in what dictators say, and the more I traveled, the more I realized that Hitler wasn't wrong about a lot of things he said. Maybe he already knew what a garbage people the Poles were, which is why he used their country as a dumping ground for dead bodies.

I am sure that if another anti-Semitic dictator came to power today, the vast majority of Poles would volunteer to cremate the murdered bodies, because they are as racist against Muslims today as they were against Jews before. It is the same anti-Semitism at work again, this time with a new scapegoat. Because the stupid always need a scapegoat to help them cope with their own incompetence as a people.

There are many things I thought about the world before I traveled and that changed when I saw reality with my own eyes. For example, I never imagined that Europe as a continent would be so horrible, but the more I traveled there, the more I understood why these people have been killing each other for thousands of years. There's a lot of stupidity in those nations.

Someone once asked me when I said this: "But aren't you European?"

Well, yes, I am, but why don't I have the right to judge the people where I come from, just because I shouldn't in the eyes of the hypocrites?

If I have a parasite in my stomach, I don't say I'm a parasite with a parasite, or that the parasite is part of me. Instead, I say I must remove this parasite in order to be healthy! In the same way, I truly believe that the world will be a better place if stupid people are identified and removed from society, as we do with dangerous criminals, even if we have to destroy many nations and scatter their people all over the planet, instead of getting rid of them with an atomic bomb, as the Americans did against Japan in the greatest demonstration of xenophobia and racism the world has ever seen.

Narcissists are not human, they are subhuman, they don't think like normal people, and they are not only mentally retarded, but very dangerous. They do not deserve the same rights as normal people, precisely because they are a cancer in the world, a disease.

A disease cannot be confused with the optimal state of health, so we can't confuse stupid people with normal people and then say it's normal to be stupid, or that there is no normal because everyone is mentally ill, as I often hear these days.

The more the stupid get into positions of power, the more they try to normalize stupidity to the detriment of everyone else.

They devalue intellectual effort and suppress reason and common sense, making everyone dumber. They also literally poison people's minds, as is now done with almost everything we find in a supermarket. But 81% of mentally ill people don't cancel out 19% of sane people by simply lying. Even if there were only 1% of sane people on the planet, we should still do our best to give them more rights and less rights to the 99% of insane people.

This should be logical, but if you disagree with me, you are basically assuming that wars are normal, genocide is normal, discrimination is normal, and the war against stupidity has no end, because that is exactly what it means to normalize stupidity in the world.

It's also how an apathetic people react to evil, by just letting it happen and finding reasons to let it happen instead of confronting it.

People who do this have learned helplessness, they've given up fighting back because they don't believe they can change the world. Everyone I confront with truths, when they admit I'm right, says, "There's nothing I can do about it!"

That is no justification except lack of responsibility, because every time you lie to protect a hypocrisy, you become part of the problem and perpetuate it.

People say this because they are afraid to confront the people they know, to be seen as antagonistic, and even to be labeled crazy. They say they can't change the world, knowing full well that they simply don't want others to know they think differently. They protest their own right to do nothing and not be seen as a problem for the stupid. They are cowards.

Here's the simplest thing you can do for the world: Share this book, promote it, tell someone else to read it. Because I may not be a politician, but I don't write these books for entertainment.

Chapter 17: Breaking the Chains of Learned Helplessness

You realize how stupid it is to think you can't do anything for the world when the stupid ruin your life because you are too honest and kind to belong to a planet full of stupid people. In fact, on such a planet, the stupid have more rights than the intelligent, kind, hardworking people, so you can actually separate these types of people into two species, because you will see two very different realities unfolding under their control.

When I used to put on parties, the DJs were always happy and would tell me, "I've never had so much fun! I could come to one of your parties even if you didn't pay me, just because I had a great experience! Why would they say that? Because there was no competition among them.

I gave everyone the opportunity to be themselves, and I would even encourage them to share their knowledge with each other. Also, even though I was the organizer, I never used them to promote myself or to take more time from them to perform, and they respected that, but they had never seen it before, because the world they knew was the world of the stupid, where all DJs compete to be the best, nobody is a friend to anybody, and in the end the only thing that counts is the money, not the fun, and even that comes with effort, because the organizer is often a bully who likes to put musicians down to make himself look more important than he is.

It's often said that stupidity is not a choice, but that's not entirely true, there's a difference between being born without skills and choosing not to use them. Stupidity is not inherent in a person, but the willingness to remain constantly uneducated and lazy, while refusing to learn from the experiences of others, refusing to be cooperative and kind to others.

That can make you a stupid person. That's why stupid people are incapable of productive dialogue; they are so blind to reality and so obsessed with themselves that they cannot see beyond their own limited and selfish perceptions.In their imaginary world, they organize words into blocks, except that because they're too stupid, they only have a few divisions to play with, and that's how they organize their minds. It's almost like they have a template that they use to organize their thoughts: "me good, others bad", "me smart, others stupid", "me special, others disposable", "me white supremacist, others poor and stupid black and brown people".

Their ability to assimilate new information is extremely low or nonexistent, which can be incredibly damaging, especially in societies still in transition to democratic governance. In such places, stupid people tend to be used by the ruling elite, who use them to undermine the democratic process of society in favor of their own interests.

Unfortunately, this is a vicious cycle that perpetuates itself to the detriment of everyone in the society. Stupid people are easily influenced by the arrogance of others who are just like them. They admire arrogant people because they are perceived as more valuable, since value to them is measured by appearance, popularity, and social status.

Instead of trusting in experience and humility, the fools often follow those who exude narcissism, so it's not uncommon for them to associate with other individuals with similar traits, even when the same individuals they admire bully them.

I believe that the stupid gravitate toward those who are like them because they lack the ability to discern a person's true worth and instead confuse worth with arrogance. They base their judgments on how they see themselves. Their obsession with appearing smart causes them to listen only to people with arrogant attitudes.

In their eyes, being overly confident means you must be knowledgeable, so they ignore those who don't try to demonstrate some form of superiority. They despise normality and common sense because they can only respect arrogance and influence or some form of power over others.

Their world is black and white, and if you are humble, you have no value to them and they will treat you with contempt. Respecting a narcissist is like downgrading yourself, because they will only insult you more. The stupid often follow what is popular without taking the time to analyze its true value. They have no capacity for discernment and assume that the majority knows what quality is.

They crave the respect of others and are afraid to accept anything that the majority might reject.

The voice of the majority is like God to them. As a result, they consume popular content, easily follow trends, and reinforce their own beliefs about themselves based on what they see others doing, even if it is idiotic or self-degrading.

Chapter 18: Why Creativity and Intelligence Go Unnoticed

The cycle of stupidity and narcissism is dangerous because it leads to a society that is so full of opinions about things that no one understands. Instead of seeking knowledge and expertise, narcissists and idiots in general focus their efforts on making others believe they know what they are talking about.

They only care about making money because they know that money gives them more power and influence, so they will go to great lengths to fool others into paying them. They don't trust knowledge, they trust results, and they only listen to those who have money to spend and control other people's opinions.

The stupid are always looking for validation and only give it to those who seem to have gained more power and control, but because they are constantly seeking the approval of others and are afraid of being rejected and ridiculed, they can't take different paths in life or accept anything new that hasn't been validated by others.

This is also why they can't be good entrepreneurs and why they lack creativity. In fact, they are just the opposite. The stupid can only copy and steal ideas from others.

Interestingly, they are so desperate for acceptance that they will change their minds at a moment's notice when they realize that the change will bring them greater admiration. One minute they are ridiculing a person, and the next minute they are asking for their opinion if they think this person can lead them to more power and knowledge.

This is why the stupid can criticize me one moment and ask me for a job an hour later, as has happened so many times in my life. All of these behaviors are symptoms of a larger problem, because the stupid are trapped in a dangerous cycle that perpetuates their own arrogance and ignorance. They only listen to those who are like them, and they don't trust anyone who doesn't have luxury cars or a large following to prove the value of what they say.

In a world like this, where the majority is so stupid, the intelligent people, the creative people, often go unnoticed. Unless such people have results that validate the stupid or skills that can be explored, they are ignored and considered inferior by them.

The minds of stupid people are driven by certain perceptions related to space, time and the physical world, but because they see limits in everything, the way stupid people perceive time can have a significant impact on their decisions, judgments and interpersonal relationships, as well as how they manage their space.

There are no dimensions or frequencies for them, so they see everyone as objects - either objects that favor them, or objects that are on their way, and objects that they must destroy.

Their space is relative to their needs, so they conquer space by dominating people, and their time for things is now. Everything in the future is relative to what they want now. Because, like an infant, they are incapable of moving away from their selfish needs. And because they see everything in the now, they judge people based on immediate gains, so they consider a person valuable or not based on what he shows in the present, not what he intends to accomplish in the future or who he was in the past.

This means that if someone used to be the president of a country but is now an ordinary citizen, he may not receive the respect and valued opinion he deserves from these stupid people.

Stupid people are not interested in long-term personal or professional relationships and tend to compete with others, which makes them see only those who can give them such an advantage in the present moment. They also tend to focus on managing the tasks at hand rather than working on long-term projects, and they lack the emotional capacity to form deep connections with others or to sustain a plan over a long period of time.

This mindset can lead to high turnover in companies run by or with a high percentage of dumb people. Obsessed with social validation, productivity is never their priority. They will only do what is necessary to get the admiration they seek, and that may mean putting more effort into partying and gossiping with their coworkers than doing actual work.

Don't think, however, that a stupid person would ever be late for work, because he knows it lowers his value in the eyes of others. But if the boss is as stupid as the stupid person expects him to be, he will judge the employees by the time they arrive at the office, not by their productivity.

In a country full of stupid people, this means that no matter how productive you are, you will be judged by how many minutes you are late, so if I am 10 minutes late, but I produce a project in one month that should take a year, I will be fired for being 10 minutes late.

In countries where the vast majority of people are too stupid, GTP is too low because everyone is obsessed with conventional norms and appearances instead of results. This is especially true in Portugal and Spain, and the reason why these countries have no future. Cultures that glorify narcissism are their own undoing.

Chapter 19: The Fleeting Motives of the Unwise

You will see that stupid people are the most involved in social activities, working hard on projects that they believe will help them gain popularity quickly or avoid losing their jobs or social status, and never missing an event or party for the same reasons. On the other hand, they get bored easily if they don't see immediate benefits.

You can't really build a team with these people or expect them to support you over time. Anything that takes longer than a few weeks is too much for them. Their motivation is only as strong as the results they see in the eyes of others in a short period of time.

When others disapprove of something, stupid people give up quickly because they measure their efforts by peer approval and their results by short-term benefits rather than long-term investment.

For example, they may prefer a job that offers high short-term financial rewards rather than sacrifice immediate benefits for long-term opportunities, but they will also sacrifice a relationship they may have had for many years, even a marriage and their children, for someone they've just met who promises immediate benefits they didn't have before.

Consistency is something we can't expect from them because they are not trustworthy. Stupid people tend to have an unstable time orientation, have difficulty with long-term tasks and commitments, and this inconsistency combined with their false promises can have various consequences, such as difficulty maintaining long-term relationships, difficulty gaining credibility, and lack of growth.

Because they have this limited view of reality, they also assume that everyone else follows the same premises, so it's not uncommon for them to expect people they've met to still be in the same places they found them, or to think others are lost or losing in life because they're no longer where they were found.

In the brain of a very stupid person, change makes no sense because everyone should be fighting in the present moment for what they have and what they can see. They have difficulty perceiving transitions over time. They cannot process the idea that someone might have decided to change countries and start over somewhere else, or give up a career because they decided to find a better one, or improve their appearance and health and gain more self-confidence.

Nothing is more confusing to the stupid person than to see someone they consider inferior progressing rapidly and getting a better life than they ever achieved for themselves, especially when they worked hard to destroy that person's future. This jealousy kills them from within.

If you really want to hurt a stupid person, achieve the things they wish they had and will never have because they are too stupid to get them, and then send them New Year's cards with your photo next to those things. Nothing makes a stupid person angrier than that.

Just imagine the face of the dean of a university in northern China who fired me because he was jealous of my popularity with the students when he realized that I was enjoying my life in Greece while he was stuck in the middle of nowhere, because by firing me he actually made me achieve my results faster. It's the same reaction family members who never helped me have when they realize I didn't need their help to have a better life than they have now.

I strongly encourage you to send them photos of you having fun, because nothing hurts them more; your success is the best revenge against stupid people. They constantly stalk you on social media and then get angry when they see you enjoying your time.

Although fear of change is a universal challenge that many people face, it is an even greater challenge for those who are stupid. Whether in their professional careers or personal lives, the anticipation of change often brings anxiety and fear, and this fear is heightened when they see others achieving what they are too afraid or incompetent to achieve on their own.

They are reluctant to take risks because they fear failure and uncertainty, and worse, the ridicule of others.

If a very stupid person suffers a setback or an illness that puts him in a hospital bed, he is very unlikely to tell anyone, especially if it could kill him, because it makes him look weak in the eyes of others. If they are permanently ill or have a terminal illness, they will simply disappear, deleting their social media or claiming it's been hacked and never using it again, leaving only their best memories, often photos taken decades ago that do not resemble their current appearance.

Chapter 20: Discovering Hidden Strengths

We live in a world where arrogance is mistaken for competence, where bullying is mistaken for strength, and where the loudest voices often drown out the wisest. But perhaps one of the most insidious aspects of stupidity is its ability to masquerade as intelligence. This false intellectualism gives the illusion of knowledge while actually reinforcing ignorance. The effects of stupidity extend far beyond individual interactions because it shapes our politics, our economies, and our cultures, which in turn shape our perceptions of the world.

It takes courage to confront these perceptions, but every challenge I've faced and every setback I've suffered has ultimately served to deepen my understanding of the complexities of life hidden beneath the layers of mass ignorance. The very people who sought to impede my progress often inadvertently propelled me forward, pushing me to explore new horizons and discover hidden strengths in opportunities I could not foresee. That's how I came to understand that true intelligence is not about accumulating facts or winning arguments, but about succeeding in life, and that success is not found in social validation, but in increasing one's wisdom and experience.

This experience in itself is nothing more than repetition over a period of time, but it can rapidly increase in value if embraced with a proactive attitude and determination. This form of experience leads to intellectual growth and maturity. It is about cultivating curiosity, embracing complexity, and keeping an open mind. It's about recognizing our own biases and limitations and constantly striving to overcome them.

One of the most important skills you will develop through experience is discernment, and in a world awash in information and misinformation, the ability to discern truth from falsehood, substance from superficiality, is crucial. This skill must be developed through exposure to diverse perspectives and a willingness to question our own assumptions. Such a quest will be met with resistance, ridicule, and even persecution, but I've found that the rewards of perseverance far outweigh the temporary discomfort of discrimination and loneliness.

As we move forward in life and witness the vast amount of change that is rapidly unfolding before our eyes, we can see that those who are stubborn about learning and have invested their efforts in maintaining the status quo can barely see or even grasp the opportunities that lie ahead, while for those who have embraced the discomfort of opposing views, change becomes a sea of opportunity to grow faster.

It was my willingness to learn and improve that kept me open to opportunities that would eventually change me in ways I could not predict or imagine. This is the true reason to continue to hope for better days to come, for fortune certainly favors the prepared mind, as I have seen in my life and in the lives of many who have followed my teachings.

The mind that is cultivated grows the fruits of intellect in the form of ideas that can determine our outcomes, the true taste of life. Happiness truly comes to those who are willing to embrace knowledge with resilience and the courage to change. Ignorance is never bliss, except for the unwise.

Combined with faith, knowledge can defy prediction and break the barriers of logic. Truly, there is no limit to what we can accomplish in life, except when we debase ourselves by trusting the voices of stupidity, the demons of nonsense that inhabit the bodies of so many of the world's fools.

While we can't reason with the unreasonable and expect them to have common sense, we can certainly rise above our baser instincts and contribute to a world that values wisdom over folly, compassion over cruelty, and truth over illusion. This optimism does not lie in blind faith in blind positivism, but rather in the ability to face uncomfortable truths about ourselves and our society. It requires us to question deeply held beliefs and behaviors, as well as norms and cultures. It requires us to cultivate patience, self-love, and perseverance in the face of disappointment.

The pursuit of knowledge, the cultivation of wisdom, and the commitment to growth are not just noble ideals; they are practical necessities for our survival and flourishing as a species. We can choose to succumb to the forces of ignorance and short-sightedness, or we can rise to the challenge of creating a more intelligent, compassionate, and sustainable world. The importance of rising above mass stupidity, however, is tied not only to the potential for a better future for humanity, but to the very essence of what it means to be human.

Chapter 21: Wisdom in Chaos

Here are the top 10 life lessons I've learned from my experience in overcoming the chaos created by the ignorant minds of the world:

1. Embrace your uniqueness: In a world that often rewards conformity, I've learned that true strength lies in embracing your uniqueness. The very qualities that make us different are often the ones that lead to our greatest achievements. I've faced ridicule, misunderstanding, and even hatred for being different, but I've come to realize that these reactions often stem from others' insecurities and limitations. By staying true to myself and my vision, I've been able to create a life that is authentically mine.

2. Turn adversity into opportunity: Life has a way of throwing unexpected challenges our way. I've learned that these obstacles, no matter how daunting, can be turned into stepping stones for growth and success. When I was fired from teaching positions or faced rejection, I used those setbacks as catalysts to pursue better opportunities. Each challenge became an opportunity to reinvent myself and push beyond my perceived limitations.

3. Knowledge is power, but wisdom is liberty: Throughout my life, I've been driven by an insatiable thirst for knowledge. However, I've come to understand that simply accumulating information is not enough. True power comes from applying that knowledge wisely and using it to navigate the complexities of life. Wisdom, I've found, is the ability to see beyond superficial appearances and understand the deeper truths that govern our world.

4. Question everything, especially authority: One of the most valuable lessons I've learned is the importance of critical thinking. In a world filled with misinformation and manipulation, it's crucial to question everything, especially those in positions of authority. Whether it's in education, healthcare, or politics, I've seen how blind acceptance of the status quo can lead to stagnation and even harm. By maintaining a healthy skepticism and always seeking the truth, we can protect ourselves from deception and make more informed decisions.

5. Cultivate resilience and self-reliance: Life has taught me the invaluable lesson of resilience. From facing homelessness to dealing with betrayal, I've learned that the ability to bounce back from adversity is essential to survival and success. Hand in hand with resilience is self-reliance. I've discovered that true freedom comes from being able to rely on myself, both mentally and financially. This self-sufficiency has allowed me to pursue my passions and live life on my own terms.

6. Embrace solitude and introspection: In a world that often equates constant social interaction with happiness, I've discovered the immense value of solitude. Some of my most profound

insights and creative ideas have come during moments of quiet contemplation. Solitude has allowed me to connect deeply with myself, process my experiences, and gain clarity about my path forward. It's in these moments of reflection that I've been able to truly understand myself and my place in the world.

7. Recognize the limitations of others: One of the hardest but most liberating lessons I've learned is recognizing and accepting the limitations of others, especially those closest to us. I've come to understand that many people, including family members and colleagues, operate from a place of fear, insecurity, or ignorance. While this realization can be painful, it's also liberating. It has allowed me to set healthier boundaries, manage my expectations, and focus my energy on those who truly support and understand me.

8. Seek growth, not validation: Early in my life, I sought validation from others, believing that external approval was the key to success and happiness. However, I've learned that true fulfillment comes from pursuing personal growth and staying true to one's values. The opinions of others, especially those who don't understand our journey, should not dictate our choices or our self-worth. By focusing on my own growth and following my passion for writing and learning, I've found a sense of purpose that no external validation could provide.

9. Embrace change and adaptability: In a rapidly changing world, I've found that adaptability is the key to not only surviving, but thriving. Whether it's changing careers, moving to new countries, or adjusting to unexpected life events, being open to change

has allowed me to seize opportunities and grow in ways I never imagined. I've learned to see change not as a threat, but as an exciting opportunity for new experiences and personal growth.

10. Never stop learning and growing: The world is constantly changing, and in order to stay relevant and fulfilled, we must constantly evolve. Whether it's acquiring new skills, exploring other cultures, or challenging our own beliefs, the pursuit of knowledge and personal growth is what keeps life exciting and meaningful.

Glossary

Adaptability: The ability to adjust to new conditions or circumstances, demonstrating flexibility and resilience in the face of change.

Altruism: The belief in or practice of selfless concern for the welfare of others, often involving acts of kindness and generosity without expectation of reward.

Anti-Semitism: Prejudice, hostility, or discrimination against Semitic peoples. Semitic peoples include Arabs, Arameans, Jews, Assyrians, Phoenicians (including modern Lebanese), Ethiopians (especially Amhara and Tigrayans), and Maltese. These groups are historically linked by their use of Semitic languages, such as Arabic, Hebrew, Amharic, and Aramaic. Anti-Semitism can manifest itself in various forms of prejudice, stereotyping, discrimination, or violence against any of these Semitic ethnic and linguistic groups. While the term has often been used specifically to refer to prejudice against Jews in recent history, its broader meaning encompasses prejudice against all Semitic peoples. Thus, it is important to recognize the diversity of groups that fall under the umbrella of Semitic peoples when discussing and addressing anti-Semitism.

Apathy: Lack of interest, enthusiasm, or concern, often characterized by indifference or lack of motivation to take action.

Arabophobia: Prejudice, hostility or discrimination against Arab people, their culture and heritage. It can take many forms, including stereotyping, prejudicial attitudes, discriminatory practices, and acts of violence. Arabophobia often involves negative perceptions and misconceptions about Arabs, their customs and beliefs, leading to unfair treatment and social exclusion.

Arrogance: An attitude of superiority manifested in an overbearing manner or presumptuous claims, often leading to a disregard for the opinions or feelings of others.

Hubris: Having or displaying an exaggerated sense of one's own importance or abilities, often accompanied by a disregard for the opinions or feelings of others.

Betrayal: The act of being disloyal or unfaithful to someone who trusts you, often involving the breaking of promises or confidences.

Bullying: The use of force, coercion, or threats to abuse, aggressively dominate, or intimidate others, often resulting in physical or emotional harm.

Chaos: A state of complete disorder and confusion, often characterized by a lack of organization, structure, or predictability.

Childish: Characteristic of, appropriate to, or resembling a child, often involving immaturity, innocence, or simplicity.

Cognitive Dissonance: The state of having inconsistent thoughts, beliefs, or attitudes, especially regarding behavioral choices and attitude changes, often resulting in psychological discomfort.

Compassion: Sympathetic concern for the suffering or misfortune of others, often accompanied by a desire to help or alleviate their distress.

Competence: The ability to do something successfully or efficiently, often involving the possession of necessary skills, knowledge, and experience.

Courage: The ability to do something that frightens one, often involving bravery, determination, and a willingness to face challenges or risks.

Creativity: The use of imagination or original ideas to create something; inventiveness, often involving the ability to think outside the box and innovate.

Critical thinking: The objective analysis and evaluation of an issue to form a judgment, often involving the use of logic, reasoning, and evidence.

Deception: The act of deceiving someone, often involving the use of lies, misinformation, or manipulation to mislead or trick others.

Depth: The quality of being deep or profound, often involving thoroughness, completeness, or detailed understanding.

Discernment: The ability to judge well and make wise decisions, especially in distinguishing truth from falsehood, often involving keen insight and perception.

Discredit: To harm the good reputation of, often involving the spreading of negative information or accusations to undermine someone's credibility or standing.

Discrimination: The unfair or prejudicial treatment of different groups of people, especially on the basis of race, age, or gender, often resulting in inequality and social injustice.

Dogma: A principle or set of principles established by authority as unquestionably true, often involving rigid adherence to beliefs or doctrines without question or doubt.

Dunning-Kruger Effect: A cognitive bias in which people with limited knowledge or competence in a particular intellectual or social domain greatly overestimate their own knowledge or competence in that domain, often leading to overconfidence and poor decision making.

Empathy: The ability to understand and share the feelings of another, often including the ability to put oneself in another's shoes and respond with compassion.

Entitlement: The belief that one is inherently deserving of privileges or special treatment, often involving a sense of superiority or disregard for the rights or needs of others.

Envy: A feeling of dissatisfaction or resentful longing aroused by someone else's possessions, qualities, or happiness, often leading to jealousy and a desire for what others have.

Experience: Practical contact with and observation of facts or events, often involving the acquisition of knowledge, skill, and wisdom through direct involvement.

Extremism: The holding of extreme political or religious views, often involving radical beliefs, intolerance, or a willingness to use violence to achieve goals.

False intellectualism: The act of presenting oneself as more intelligent or knowledgeable than one actually is, often involving the use of jargon, pretentious language, or superficial understanding.

Fluoride: A chemical compound commonly added to public water supplies and dental products such as toothpaste and mouthwash that has negative effects on cognitive function, not only in children but also in adults. Higher levels of fluoride exposure have been associated with lower IQ scores and impaired neurological development in children. It has also been linked to cognitive decline, memory problems, and other neurological problems in older populations.

Fluorine: A highly reactive, pale yellow gas that is the lightest member of the halogen family. Fluorine is known for its extreme reactivity, making it one of the most reactive elements. It is commonly used in various chemical compounds, including fluoride, which is added to water supplies and dental products. However, fluorine and its compounds have potential adverse health effects.

Fraud: Wrongful or criminal deception intended to result in financial or personal gain, often involving the use of deception, misrepresentation, or manipulation.

Gaslighting: A form of psychological manipulation in which a person or group sows seeds of doubt that cause them to question their own memory, perception, and sanity, often leading to confusion and self-doubt.

Genocide: The deliberate killing of a large group of people, especially those of a particular ethnic group or nation, often involving systematic and widespread violence.

Groupthink: The practice of thinking or making decisions as a group, typically resulting in unquestioned, poor-quality decisions, often due to a desire for harmony or conformity within the group.

Growth: The process of increasing in physical size, quantity, or value, often involving development, maturation, or expansion.

Hate: Intense dislike or ill will, often involving strong negative emotions and a desire to harm or belittle others.

Homelessness: The state of having no home or permanent residence, often involving poverty, social isolation, and lack of basic necessities.

Humility: The quality of having a modest or low view of one's importance, often involving selflessness, respect for others, and a willingness to learn and grow.

Hypocrisy: The practice of claiming to have moral standards or beliefs with which one's own behavior does not conform, often involving deceit and a lack of integrity.

Ignorance: Lack of knowledge or information, often resulting from a lack of education, experience, or exposure to new ideas.

Incompetence: The inability to do something successfully; ineptitude, often involving a lack of skills, knowledge, or experience necessary to perform a task effectively.

Indoctrination: The process of teaching an individual or group to accept a set of beliefs uncritically, often involving the use of propaganda, persuasion, or coercion to inculcate certain values or ideologies.

Insecurity: Uncertainty or fear about oneself; lack of confidence, often involving self-doubt, fear of failure, or feelings of inferiority.

Integrity: The quality of being honest and having strong moral principles, often involving ethical behavior, reliability, and a commitment to doing the right thing.

Intellectual Curiosity: A strong desire to learn, understand, and explore new ideas and concepts, often involving a passion for knowledge and a willingness to question and investigate.

Intelligence: The ability to acquire and apply knowledge and skills, often involving reasoning, problem solving, and critical thinking.

Introspection: The examination or observation of one's own mental and emotional processes, often involving self-reflection and a desire to understand oneself.

Invalidation: The act of declaring or making something invalid, often involving the rejection, dismissal, or undermining of someone's feelings, opinions, or experiences.

Islamophobia: Prejudice, hostility, or discrimination against Muslims or the religion of Islam. It can take many forms, including stereotyping, prejudicial attitudes, discriminatory practices, and acts of violence. Islamophobia often involves negative perceptions and misconceptions about Muslims and their beliefs, leading to unfair treatment, social exclusion and marginalization of Muslim communities. It can also include the demonization of Islamic practices, texts, and symbols.

Jealousy: Feeling or showing envy of someone or their accomplishments and advantages, often involving resentment and a desire for what others have.

Learned Helplessness: A condition in which a person suffers from a sense of powerlessness resulting from persistent failure to succeed, often leading to a lack of motivation and a belief that one's actions have no effect on outcomes.

Loneliness: Sadness due to a lack of friends or companionship, often accompanied by feelings of isolation, emptiness, or a desire for social connection. It is also the state or situation of being alone, often involving isolation, introspection, or the desire for privacy and quiet reflection.

Manipulation: The act of manipulating someone in a clever or unscrupulous way, often involving the use of deception, coercion, or emotional pressure to control or influence others.

Mediocrity: The quality or state of being mediocre, often involving a lack of excellence, distinction, or notable achievement.

Misinformation: False or inaccurate information, especially that which is deliberately intended to deceive, often leading to confusion, misunderstanding, or harmful consequences.

Narcissism: Excessive interest in or admiration of one's self and physical appearance, often accompanied by a grandiose sense of self-importance and a lack of empathy for others.

Narcissistic abuse: A form of emotional abuse inflicted by someone with narcissistic personality traits, often involving manipulation, control, and a disregard for the feelings and needs of others.

Neurotoxin: A poison that affects the nervous system, often damaging nerve cells and interfering with the transmission of nerve impulses.

Objectivity: The quality of being objective, unbiased, and impartial, often involving the ability to consider facts and evidence without personal bias or emotion.

Oppression: Prolonged cruel or unfair treatment or control, often involving the systematic mistreatment, discrimination, or exploitation of a group or individual.

Paranoia: Unjustified suspicion and distrust of other people, often involving delusional beliefs, irrational fears, or a sense of persecution.

Persecution: Hostility and mistreatment, especially based on race or political or religious beliefs, often involving discrimination, harassment, or violence.

Perseverance: Persistence in doing something despite difficulties or delays in achieving success, often involving determination, resilience, and a willingness to overcome obstacles.

Prejudice: A preconceived opinion not based on reason or actual experience, often involving biased attitudes or discriminatory behavior toward certain groups or individuals.

Propaganda: Information, especially of a biased or misleading nature, used to promote a political cause or point of view, often involving the manipulation of public opinion or the dissemination of disinformation.

Provocation: Action or speech that offends someone, especially intentionally, often with the intent to provoke a reaction or response.

Psychological Abuse: A form of abuse characterized by one person subjecting or exposing another person to behavior that may result in psychological trauma, often involving emotional manipulation, verbal attacks, or threats.

Psychopath: A person suffering from a chronic mental disorder with abnormal or violent social behavior, often involving a lack of empathy, remorse, or concern for the welfare of others.

Racism: Prejudice, discrimination, or antagonism directed against a person or persons on the basis of race or ethnicity, often involving systemic inequalities and social injustice.

Rationalization: The act of attempting to explain or justify behavior or an attitude with logical reasons, even when they are not appropriate, often involving the use of excuses or self-deception to avoid responsibility.

Resentment: Bitter indignation at having been treated unfairly, often involving feelings of anger, frustration, or desire for retribution.

Resilience: The ability to recover quickly from difficulties; toughness, often involving the ability to bounce back from adversity and maintain a positive outlook.

Scapegoat: A person blamed for the misdeeds, mistakes, or faults of others, often involving the transfer of blame or responsibility to an innocent party.

Self-Knowledge: Conscious knowledge of one's character, feelings, motives, and desires, often involving self-reflection and a deep understanding of one's strengths and weaknesses.

Self-esteem: Confidence in one's worth or abilities; self-respect, often involving a positive self-image and a sense of personal worth.

Self-fulfilling prophecy: A prediction that comes true because of the believer's behavior, often involving the influence of expectations on outcomes.

Self-reliance: Relying on one's own strengths and resources rather than those of others, often involving independence, self-sufficiency, and a sense of personal responsibility.

Self-sabotage: The action or inaction taken to undermine one's own efforts or goals, often involving self-destructive behavior, procrastination, or a lack of self-confidence.

Skepticism: A skeptical attitude; doubt about the truth of something, often involving a critical examination of evidence and a questioning of accepted beliefs or claims.

Slander: The act or crime of making a false spoken statement that damages a person's reputation, often involving defamation and a violation of a person's rights.

Social Validation: Approval from others that influences a person's thoughts, feelings, and behaviors, often involving a desire for acceptance, conformity, or a sense of belonging.

Stigma: A mark of disgrace associated with a particular circumstance, quality, or person, often involving social judgment, discrimination, or negative perception.

Stupidity: Behavior that shows a lack of good sense or judgment, often discussed in the book as a societal problem involving poor decision making and a failure to think critically.

Superficiality: Lack of thoroughness, depth of character, or serious thought, often involving a focus on appearances, trivial matters, or a shallow understanding of issues.

Survival Instinct: An innate behavior that allows people and animals to protect themselves from harm, often involving self-preservation and a strong desire to live.

Toxic Personality: A person who is harmful to others through their negative behaviors and attitudes, often involving manipulation, criticism, or emotional abuse.

Trauma: A deeply distressing or disturbing experience, often involving physical or emotional harm, psychological distress, or a lasting impact on one's well-being.

Tribalism: The behaviors and attitudes that result from strong loyalty to one's tribe or social group, often including a sense of belonging, identity, and a willingness to defend or support one's group.

Tyranny: Cruel and oppressive government or rule, often involving abuse of power, suppression of rights, and use of force to maintain control.

Uniqueness: The quality of being unlike anything else; being the only one of its kind, often involving individuality, originality, or a distinctive character.

Validation: Recognition or affirmation that a person or their feelings or opinions are valid or worthwhile, often involving support, encouragement, and a sense of being valued.

Victimhood: The state of having been hurt, harmed, or made to suffer, often involving a sense of powerlessness, vulnerability, or a desire for justice or compensation.

Vulnerability: The quality or state of being exposed to the possibility of being attacked or harmed, either physically or emotionally, often involving a sense of openness, sensitivity, or need for protection.

Wisdom: The quality of having experience, knowledge, and good judgment, often involving the ability to make sound decisions and provide insightful guidance.

Xenophobia: Dislike of or prejudice against people from other countries, often involving fear, hostility, or discrimination against foreigners.

Zeitgeist: The defining spirit or mood of a particular period in history as expressed in the ideas and beliefs of the time, often reflecting the cultural, political, and social climate.

Bibliography

Choi, A. L., Sun, G., Zhang, Y., & Grandjean, P. (2012). Developmental fluoride neurotoxicity: A systematic review and meta-analysis. Environmental Health Perspectives, 120(10), 1362-1368.

Derendorf, H., Hochhaus, G., Meibohm, B., Möllmann, H., & Barth, J. (1995). Pharmacokinetics and pharmacodynamics of inhaled corticosteroids. Journal of Allergy and Clinical Immunology, 96(5), 729-740.

Guan, Z. Z., Wang, Y. N., Xiao, K. Q., Dai, D. Y., Chen, Y. H., Liu, J. L., ... & Shen, Y. M. (1998). Influence of chronic fluorosis on membrane lipids in rat brain. Neurotoxicology and Teratology, 20(5), 537-542.

Luke, J. (2001). Fluoride deposition in the aged human pineal gland. Caries Research, 35(2), 125-128.

Mazze, R. I., Callan, C. M., Galvez, S. T., Delgado-Herrera, L., & Mayer, D. B. (1992). The effects of sevoflurane on serum creatinine and blood urea nitrogen concentrations: A retrospective, twenty-two-center, comparative evaluation of renal function in adult surgical patients. Anesthesia & Analgesia, 75(4S), S4-S12.

Remitly. (2023). Q4 and Full Year 2022 Results. [Corporate financial report].

Till, C., Green, R., Grundy, J. G., Hornung, R., Neufeld, R., Martinez-Mier, E. A., ... & Lanphear, B. P. (2015). Community water fluoridation and urinary fluoride concentrations in a national sample of pregnant women in Canada. Environmental Health Perspectives, 126(10), 107001.

Additional sources:

Federal Bureau of Investigation (FBI). (n.d.). Annual crime statistics. [Referenced for robbery homicide statistics]

National Highway Traffic Safety Administration (NHTSA). (n.d.). Annual pedestrian fatality reports. [Referenced for pedestrian death statistics]

Book Review Request

Dear reader,

Thank you for purchasing this book! I would love to know your opinion. Writing a book review helps in understanding the readers and also impacts other readers' purchasing decisions. Your opinion matters. Please write a book review!

Your kindness is greatly appreciated!

About the Author

Dan Desmarques is a renowned author with a remarkable track record in the literary world. With an impressive portfolio of 28 Amazon bestsellers, including eight #1 bestsellers, Dan is a respected figure in the industry. Drawing on his background as a college professor of academic and creative writing, as well as his experience as a seasoned business consultant, Dan brings a unique blend of expertise to his work. His profound insights and transformational content appeal to a wide audience, covering topics as diverse as personal growth, success, spirituality, and the deeper meaning of life. Through his writing, Dan empowers readers to break free from limitations, unlock their inner potential, and embark on a journey of self-discovery and transformation. In a competitive self-help market, Dan's exceptional talent and inspiring stories make him a standout author, motivating readers to engage with his books and embark on a path of personal growth and enlightenment.

Also Written by the Author

1. 66 Days to Change Your Life: 12 Steps to Effortlessly Remove Mental Blocks, Reprogram Your Brain and Become a Money Magnet

2. A New Way of Being: How to Rewire Your Brain and Take Control of Your Life

3. Abnormal: How to Train Yourself to Think Differently and Permanently Overcome Evil Thoughts

4. Alignment: The Process of Transmutation Within the Mechanics of Life

5. Audacity: How to Make Fast and Efficient Decisions in Any Situation

6. Breaking Free from Samsara: Achieving Spiritual Liberation and Inner Peace

7. Breakthrough: Embracing Your True Potential in a

Changing World

8. Christ Cult Codex: The Untold Secrets of the Abrahamic Religions and the Cult of Jesus

9. Codex Illuminatus: Quotes & Sayings of Dan Desmarques

10. Collective Consciousness: How to Transcend Mass Consciousness and Become One With the Universe

11. Creativity: Everything You Always Wanted to Know About How to Use Your Imagination to Create Original Art That People Admire

12. Deception: When Everything You Know about God is Wrong

13. Demigod: What Happens When You Transcend The Human Nature?

14. Discernment: How Do Your Emotions Affect Moral Decision-Making?

15. Design Your Dream Life: A Guide to Living Purposefully

16. Eclipsing Mediocrity: How to Unveil Hidden Realities and Master Life's Challenges

17. Energy Vampires: How to Identify and Protect Yourself

18. Fearless: Powerful Ways to Get Abundance Flowing into Your Life

19. Feel, Think and Grow Rich: 4 Elements to Attract Success in Life

20. Find Your Flow: How to Get Wisdom and Knowledge from God

21. Hacking the Universe: The Revolutionary Way to Achieve Your Dreams and Unleash Your True Power

22. Holistic Psychology: 77 Secrets about the Mind That They Don't Want You to Know

23. How to Change the World: The Path of Global Ascension Through Consciousness

24. How to Get Lucky: How to Change Your Mind and Get Anything in Life

25. How to Improve Your Self-Esteem: 34 Essential Life Lessons Everyone Should Learn to Find Genuine Happiness

26. How to Study and Understand Anything: Discovering The Secrets of the Greatest Geniuses in History

27. Intuition: 5 Keys to Awaken Your Third Eye and Expand Spiritual Perception

28. Legacy: How to Build a Life Worth Remembering

29. Master Your Emotions: The Art of Intentional Living

30. Mastering Alchemy: The Key to Success and Spiritual

Growth

31. Metanoia Mechanics: The Secret Science of Profound Mental Shifts

32. Metamorphosis: 16 Catalysts for Unconventional Growth and Transformation

33. Mindshift: Aligning Your Thoughts for a Better Life

34. Mind Over Madness: Strategies for Thriving Amidst Chaos

35. Money Matters: A Holistic Approach to Building Financial Freedom and Well-Being

36. Religious Leadership: The 8 Rules Behind Successful Congregations

37. Reset: How to Observe Life Through the Hidden Dimensions of Reality and Change Your Destiny

38. Resilience: The Art of Confronting Reality Against the Odds

39. Raise Your Frequency: Aligning with Higher Consciousness

40. Revelation: The War Between Wisdom and Human Perception

41. Singularity: What to Do When You Lose Hope in Everything

42. Spiritual Warfare: What You Need to Know About Overcoming Adversity

43. Starseed: Secret Teachings about Heaven and the Future of Humanity

44. Stupid People: Identifying, Analyzing and Overcoming Their Toxic Influence

45. Technocracy: The New World Order of the Illuminati and The Battle Between Good and Evil

46. The 10 Laws of Transmutation: The Multidimensional Power of Your Subconscious Mind

47. The 14 Karmic Laws of Love: How to Develop a Healthy and Conscious Relationship With Your Soulmate

48. The 33 Laws of Persistence: How to Overcome Obstacles and Upgrade Your Mindset for Success

49. The 36 Laws of Happiness: How to Solve Urgent Problems and Create a Better Future

50. The Alchemy of Truth: Embracing Change and Transcending Time

51. The Altruistic Edge: Succeeding by Putting Others First

52. The Antagonists: What Makes a Successful Person Different?

53. The Antichrist: The Grand Plan of Total Global

Enslavement

54. The Art of Letting Go: Embracing Uncertainty and Living a Fulfilling Life

55. The Awakening: How to Turn Darkness Into Light and Ascend to Higher Dimensions of Existence

56. The Egyptian Mysteries: Essential Hermetic Teachings for a Complete Spiritual Reformation

57. The Dark Side of Progress: Navigating the Pitfalls of Technology and Society

58. The Evil Within: The Spiritual Battle in Your Mind Deception: When Everything You Know about God is Wrong

59. The Game of Life and How to Play It: How to Get Anything You Want in Life

60. The Hidden Language of God: How to Find a Balance Between Freedom and Responsibility

61. The Most Powerful Quotes: 400 Motivational Quotes and Sayings

62. The Secret Beliefs of The Illuminati: The Complete Truth About Manifesting Money Using The Law of Attraction That is Being Hidden From You

63. The Secret Empire: The Hidden Truth Behind the Power

Elite and the Knights of the New World Order

64. The Secret Science of the Soul: How to Transcend Common Sense and Get What You Really Want From Life

65. The Spiritual Laws of Money: The 31 Best-kept Secrets to Life-long Abundance

66. The Spiritual Mechanics of Love: Secrets They Don't Want You to Know about Understanding and Processing Emotions

67. The Unknown: Exploring Infinite Possibilities in a Conformist World

68. The Narcissist's Secret: Why They Hate You (and What to Do About It)

69. Thrive: Spark Creativity, Overcome Obstacles and Unleash Your Potential

70. Transcend: Embracing Change and Overcoming Life's Challenges

71. Uncompromised: The Surprising Power of Integrity in a Corrupt World

72. Unacknowledged: How Negative Emotions Affect Your Mental Health?

73. Unapologetic: Taking Control of Your Mind for a

Happier and Healthier Life

74. Unbreakable: Turning Hardship into Opportunity

75. Uncommon: Transcending the Lies of the Mental Health Industry

76. Unlocked: How to Get Answers from Your Subconscious Mind and Control Your Life

77. Your Full Potential: How to Overcome Fear and Solve Any Problem

78. Your Soul Purpose: Reincarnation and the Spectrum of Consciousness in Human Evolution

About the Publisher

This book was published by 22 Lions Publishing.

www.22Lions.com